# GRADE 5
# MATH FLUENCY

Peggy McLean and Lyle Lee Jenkins

*Perfect School Collection*™

To contact the authors regarding keynotes, workshops or bulk orders, visit LtoJ.net/Contact

ISBN: 978-1-956457-57-5

Book Design & Graphics: Christy Courtright, Christy's Customs LLC
Quality Assurance Manager: Kelly Lippert
Publishing Consultant: Martha Bullen, Bullen Publishing Services
Distribution Coordinator: Maggie McLaughlin

Printed in the United States of America

**The Perfect School Collection™**

*How to Create a Perfect School* by Lyle Lee Jenkins

*How to Create a Perfect Home School* by Lyle Lee Jenkins and Kelly Hawkinson Lippert

**Perfect School Collection™ Resources**

*How to Create Math Experts* series by Peggy McLean and Lyle Lee Jenkins

*How to Create Language Experts* by Codi Hrouda and Emma McInerney with Lyle Lee Jenkins

*How to Create Math Experts with Standards Quizzes* by Peggy McLean and Lyle Lee Jenkins

*How to Create a Math Foundation for Future Math Experts* by Lyle Lee Jenkins

*How to Create Bible Experts: Genesis to Revelation* by Richard Douglas Junior Jenkins with Lyle Lee Jenkins

**Early Readers**

*Bible Patterns for Young Readers* series by Lyle Lee Jenkins

*Aesop Patterns for Young Readers* series by Lyle Lee Jenkins

**Young Authors**

*Wordless Books for Young Authors* series by Jim Chansler and Lyle Lee Jenkins

**Special Project**

*All About Henry: Rich Widower of Savannah Valley* by Lyle Lee Jenkins

# INTRODUCTION
# AND
# DIRECTIONS

A perfect education occurs when the love of learning children bring with them to kindergarten is maintained until at least high school graduation. Reflect back to your youth or ask current high school students, "How many of your friends are as excited about learning in school as they once were in kindergarten?" The answers are usually below ten percent. Everyone can do better - classrooms and home schools.

What is in the process of education that causes so much discouragement among children? One of the major reasons for this loss of enthusiasm for learning is the use of data (numbers) to evaluate student learning. Data are often used in harmful ways. The purpose of data should not be to inspect the children, but to encourage them and gain insight regarding what should be done next to improve learning and joy even more. Both the Math Fluency and the Math Standards Quizzes are designed to maintain kindergarten levels of joyful learning.

Holding true to our "No Permission to Forget" slogan, we have implemented a fundamental key to knowledge retention with every quiz - review/preview. Each quiz features questions from previous grade levels and additionally questions that are a preview of content yet to be taught.

# The process behind these quizzes follows these steps:

1.  Students are shown what they are expected to know at the end of the school year.

    a.  For Math Standards Quizzes, the list of Key Concepts is provided with the *How to Create Math Experts with Math Standards Quizzes* book.

    b.  For math fluency, looking over any of the 28 quizzes included in *How to Create Math Experts with Math Fluency Quizzes* will show students what they are expected to complete in two minutes.

2.  Students take their first quiz. They may be disappointed with missing so many and are told or reminded that these quizzes are designed to show progress toward learning over the <u>whole</u> school year.

3.  Students graph the number of questions correct on a Student Run Chart that is included with the quizzes. The LtoJ system consists of 28 quizzes per year, which is 7 times a quarter.

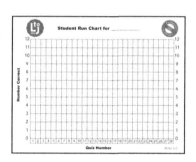

4.  In classrooms, the total number of correct answers from the whole class are added up and displayed on a Class Run Chart.

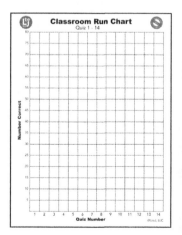

5. For home school the total correct on all quizzes from both multiple subjects and often multiple children is graphed on the Family Run Chart.

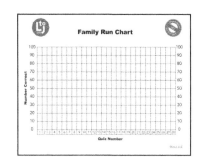

6. Students soon learn they are not expected to have 100% until late in the school year. What they are taught to look for is doing better than ever before. This is called ATB or "All Time Best." When students have more correct than ever before, a designation appears on the graph. It can be the letters ATB, a handwritten star or a sticker. Special stickers are available with the LtoJ logo or "No Permission to Forget" - please contact info@ltoj.net.

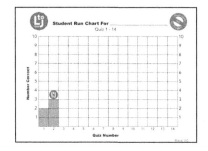

7. When families or classrooms have more correct than ever before the sticker designates the improvement and there are classroom/family celebrations.

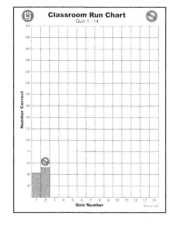

8. It is important that nothing is given to the students for their "All Time Best." Instead of giving them trinkets, students are given a memory of something fun they did every time the group had an ATB.

9. For classrooms there are more graphs for students to complete. They are the Scatter Diagram, Histogram, and Item Analysis Charts. This sounds like more work for the teacher, but since students produce the graphs it engages more students and creates even more team efforts to help each other. All these free graphs are located at www.ltoj.net. These graphs have been used since the early 2000's for all subjects and in all grade levels plus some university classrooms. The process is not limited to mathematics.

10. Some students have an especially tough time with the timed fluency quizzes. One way to create early success with timed quizzes is to have students complete the whole quiz and graph the time. An ATB occurs when less time is used than ever before. This adjustment is particularly useful in special education classrooms.

11. When students answer all questions correctly seven times in a row, they "test out" and are accelerated to the next grade level quizzes. Their contribution to the Class Run Chart is the total from the "tested out" quiz plus the new quiz.

12. For the math standards quizzes, students note the concept number on the quiz and find the corresponding concept on their Key Concept List. They highlight the concept with various colors of highlighters and then place tally marks after the statements indicating how many times they answered the concept question correctly.

---

Numbers
1. Match the number of objects with a written numeral.
2. Count to 120, starting at any number less than 120.   𝍷𝍷𝍷𝍷𝍷
3. The two digits of a two-digit number represent the number of tens and the number of ones

---

When data are for joy, so much about classrooms and home schools changes for the better. It is worth cementing in our minds the three rhyming words from John Hattie: skill, will and thrill. We want children to attain new math skills. In addition, we want their thrill to come from the successful learning evidenced by ATBs, and we want children to learn that it is effort (will) that creates the skill and thrill.

We are thrilled you have chosen to partner with LtoJ, LLC for your students' education.
Please refer to our website, www.LtoJ.net, for further resources and guidance.

$$\begin{array}{r} 9 \\ \times\ 3 \\ \hline \end{array}$$

$$\frac{2}{9} = \frac{18}{\phantom{0}}$$

$$16 \div 8 =$$

$$\begin{array}{r} 7 \\ \times\ 2 \\ \hline \end{array}$$

$$\begin{array}{r} 12 \\ \times\ 12 \\ \hline \end{array}$$

---

$$\begin{array}{r} 8 \\ +\ 6 \\ \hline \end{array}$$

$$\begin{array}{r} 8 \\ \times\ 8 \\ \hline \end{array}$$

$$\frac{1}{10} = \frac{\phantom{0}}{100}$$

$$\frac{9}{3} =$$

$$\frac{3}{10} = \frac{\phantom{0}}{40}$$

---

$$\frac{8}{9} = \frac{24}{\phantom{0}}$$

$$18 \div 6 =$$

$$\begin{array}{r} 11 \\ -\ 4 \\ \hline \end{array}$$

$$\begin{array}{r} 8 \\ +\ 8 \\ \hline \end{array}$$

$$1\overline{)5}\ =$$

---

$$\begin{array}{r} 17 \\ -\ 8 \\ \hline \end{array}$$

$$\begin{array}{r} 15 \\ +\ 2 \\ \hline \end{array}$$

$$\frac{32}{8} =$$

$$\frac{1}{12} = \frac{3}{\phantom{0}}$$

$$\begin{array}{r} 26 \\ -\ 2 \\ \hline \end{array}$$

---

$$6\overline{)48}\ =$$

$$\frac{5}{7} = \frac{35}{\phantom{0}}$$

$$\begin{array}{r} 12 \\ +\ 6 \\ \hline \end{array}$$

$$\begin{array}{r} 6 \\ \times\ 8 \\ \hline \end{array}$$

$$\begin{array}{r} 7 \\ \times\ 9 \\ \hline \end{array}$$

---

$$\begin{array}{r} 9 \\ +\ 6 \\ \hline \end{array}$$

$$\begin{array}{r} 27 \\ -\ 5 \\ \hline \end{array}$$

$$\begin{array}{r} 7 \\ \times\ 7 \\ \hline \end{array}$$

$$\begin{array}{r} 3 \\ -\ 2 \\ \hline \end{array}$$

$$\frac{4}{9} = \frac{16}{\phantom{0}}$$

---

$$\begin{array}{r} 7 \\ \times\ 0 \\ \hline \end{array}$$

$$\frac{40}{5} =$$

$$\frac{6}{13} = \frac{\phantom{0}}{39}$$

$$7\overline{)56}\ =$$

$$\begin{array}{r} 5 \\ +\ 7 \\ \hline \end{array}$$

---

$$\frac{7}{12} = \frac{\phantom{0}}{48}$$

$$\begin{array}{r} 18 \\ -\ 9 \\ \hline \end{array}$$

$$\begin{array}{r} 5 \\ \times\ 7 \\ \hline \end{array}$$

$$15 \div 3 =$$

$$\frac{9}{14} = \frac{\phantom{0}}{42}$$

Name: _____

$$\begin{array}{r} 5 \\ \times\ 5 \\ \hline \end{array}$$

$$\frac{4}{5} = \frac{16}{\phantom{16}}$$

$$8 \div 1 =$$

$$\begin{array}{r} 4 \\ \times\ 3 \\ \hline \end{array}$$

$$\begin{array}{r} 8 \\ \times\ 7 \\ \hline \end{array}$$

$$\begin{array}{r} 4 \\ +\ 9 \\ \hline \end{array}$$

$$\begin{array}{r} 8 \\ \times\ 3 \\ \hline \end{array}$$

$$\frac{1}{3} = \frac{4}{\phantom{4}}$$

$$\frac{35}{5} =$$

$$\frac{7}{9} = \frac{\phantom{63}}{63}$$

$$\frac{\phantom{1}}{\phantom{1}} = \frac{6}{12}$$

$$25 \div 5 =$$

$$\begin{array}{r} 14 \\ -\ 5 \\ \hline \end{array}$$

$$\begin{array}{r} 4 \\ +\ 6 \\ \hline \end{array}$$

$$6\overline{)24} =$$

$$\begin{array}{r} 13 \\ -\ 6 \\ \hline \end{array}$$

$$\begin{array}{r} 13 \\ +\ 4 \\ \hline \end{array}$$

$$\frac{4}{2} =$$

$$\frac{8}{11} = \frac{\phantom{33}}{33}$$

$$\begin{array}{r} 9 \\ -\ 5 \\ \hline \end{array}$$

$$2\overline{)10} =$$

$$\frac{7}{10} = \frac{\phantom{40}}{40}$$

$$\begin{array}{r} 11 \\ +\ 3 \\ \hline \end{array}$$

$$\begin{array}{r} 6 \\ \times\ 5 \\ \hline \end{array}$$

$$\begin{array}{r} 1 \\ \times\ 1 \\ \hline \end{array}$$

$$\begin{array}{r} 6 \\ +\ 6 \\ \hline \end{array}$$

$$\begin{array}{r} 7 \\ -\ 4 \\ \hline \end{array}$$

$$\begin{array}{r} 6 \\ \times\ 6 \\ \hline \end{array}$$

$$\begin{array}{r} 15 \\ -\ 4 \\ \hline \end{array}$$

$$\frac{5}{6} = \frac{\phantom{42}}{42}$$

$$\begin{array}{r} 9 \\ \times\ 6 \\ \hline \end{array}$$

$$\frac{49}{7} =$$

$$\frac{9}{\phantom{9}} = \frac{81}{90}$$

$$8\overline{)24} =$$

$$\begin{array}{r} 10 \\ +\ 10 \\ \hline \end{array}$$

$$\frac{3}{\phantom{3}} = \frac{6}{14}$$

$$\begin{array}{r} 19 \\ -\ 5 \\ \hline \end{array}$$

$$\begin{array}{r} 9 \\ \times\ 4 \\ \hline \end{array}$$

$$15 \div 5 =$$

$$\frac{2}{3} = \frac{\phantom{15}}{15}$$

$\begin{array}{r} 7 \\ \times\ 8 \\ \hline \end{array}$

$\dfrac{4}{11} = \dfrac{16}{\phantom{00}}$

$36 \div 6 =$

$\begin{array}{r} 6 \\ \times\ 5 \\ \hline \end{array}$

$\begin{array}{r} 6 \\ \times\ 2 \\ \hline \end{array}$


$\begin{array}{r} 13 \\ +\ 5 \\ \hline \end{array}$

$\begin{array}{r} 7 \\ \times\ 3 \\ \hline \end{array}$

$\dfrac{6}{11} = \dfrac{54}{\phantom{00}}$

$\dfrac{12}{2} =$

$\dfrac{3}{8} = \dfrac{\phantom{0}}{32}$


$\dfrac{8}{15} = \dfrac{16}{\phantom{00}}$

$18 \div 6 =$

$\begin{array}{r} 16 \\ -\ 7 \\ \hline \end{array}$

$\begin{array}{r} 17 \\ +\ 2 \\ \hline \end{array}$

$9\overline{)63}\ =$


$\begin{array}{r} 12 \\ -\ 5 \\ \hline \end{array}$

$\begin{array}{r} 6 \\ +\ 8 \\ \hline \end{array}$

$\dfrac{15}{5} =$

$\dfrac{3}{10} = \dfrac{9}{\phantom{00}}$

$\begin{array}{r} 19 \\ -\ 4 \\ \hline \end{array}$


$5\overline{)30}\ =$

$\dfrac{\phantom{0}}{\phantom{0}} = \dfrac{18}{28}$  (numerator 9)

$\begin{array}{r} 4 \\ +\ 7 \\ \hline \end{array}$

$\begin{array}{r} 7 \\ \times\ 7 \\ \hline \end{array}$

$\begin{array}{r} 5 \\ \times\ 4 \\ \hline \end{array}$


$\begin{array}{r} 9 \\ +\ 8 \\ \hline \end{array}$

$\begin{array}{r} 12 \\ -\ 7 \\ \hline \end{array}$

$\begin{array}{r} 8 \\ \times\ 9 \\ \hline \end{array}$

$\begin{array}{r} 14 \\ -\ 8 \\ \hline \end{array}$

$\dfrac{5}{\phantom{0}} = \dfrac{25}{55}$


$\begin{array}{r} 4 \\ \times\ 4 \\ \hline \end{array}$

$\dfrac{81}{9} =$

$\dfrac{1}{4} = \dfrac{5}{\phantom{00}}$

$2\overline{)14}\ =$

$\begin{array}{r} 2 \\ +\ 3 \\ \hline \end{array}$


$\dfrac{7}{8} = \dfrac{56}{\phantom{00}}$

$\begin{array}{r} 17 \\ -\ 3 \\ \hline \end{array}$

$\begin{array}{r} 2 \\ \times\ 2 \\ \hline \end{array}$

$12 \div 3 =$

$\dfrac{1}{5} = \dfrac{8}{\phantom{00}}$

$$
\begin{array}{r} 9 \\ \times\ 9 \\ \hline \end{array}
\qquad
\frac{5}{8} = \frac{15}{\quad}
\qquad
6 \div 3 =
\qquad
\begin{array}{r} 7 \\ \times\ 7 \\ \hline \end{array}
\qquad
\begin{array}{r} 9 \\ \times\ 6 \\ \hline \end{array}
$$

$$
\begin{array}{r} 4 \\ +\ 8 \\ \hline \end{array}
\qquad
\begin{array}{r} 8 \\ \times\ 0 \\ \hline \end{array}
\qquad
\frac{6}{17} = \frac{12}{\quad}
\qquad
\frac{45}{9} =
\qquad
\frac{5}{7} = \frac{\quad}{35}
$$

$$
\frac{\quad}{\ } = \frac{3}{18}
\qquad
28 \div 4 =
\qquad
\begin{array}{r} 34 \\ -\ 3 \\ \hline \end{array}
\qquad
\begin{array}{r} 16 \\ +\ 3 \\ \hline \end{array}
\qquad
7\overline{)28} =
$$

$$
\begin{array}{r} 21 \\ -\ 2 \\ \hline \end{array}
\qquad
\begin{array}{r} 17 \\ +\ 4 \\ \hline \end{array}
\qquad
\frac{21}{3} =
\qquad
\frac{9}{21} = \frac{3}{\quad}
\qquad
\begin{array}{r} 17 \\ -\ 6 \\ \hline \end{array}
$$

$$
3\overline{)9} =
\qquad
\frac{\quad}{5} = \frac{9}{15}
\qquad
\begin{array}{r} 7 \\ +\ 9 \\ \hline \end{array}
\qquad
\begin{array}{r} 8 \\ \times\ 9 \\ \hline \end{array}
\qquad
\begin{array}{r} 9 \\ \times\ 3 \\ \hline \end{array}
$$

$$
\begin{array}{r} 9 \\ +\ 3 \\ \hline \end{array}
\qquad
\begin{array}{r} 15 \\ -\ 7 \\ \hline \end{array}
\qquad
\begin{array}{r} 3 \\ \times\ 3 \\ \hline \end{array}
\qquad
\begin{array}{r} 13 \\ -\ 6 \\ \hline \end{array}
\qquad
\frac{6}{7} = \frac{24}{\quad}
$$

$$
\begin{array}{r} 7 \\ \times\ 6 \\ \hline \end{array}
\qquad
\frac{18}{6} =
\qquad
\frac{2}{11} = \frac{6}{\quad}
\qquad
6\overline{)42} =
\qquad
\begin{array}{r} 9 \\ +\ 9 \\ \hline \end{array}
$$

$$
\frac{2}{9} = \frac{4}{\quad}
\qquad
\begin{array}{r} 22 \\ -\ 11 \\ \hline \end{array}
\qquad
\begin{array}{r} 7 \\ \times\ 4 \\ \hline \end{array}
\qquad
27 \div 9 =
\qquad
\frac{\quad}{\ } = \frac{3}{27}
$$

$\begin{array}{r} 8 \\ \times\ 6 \\ \hline \end{array}$

$\dfrac{8}{9} = \dfrac{32}{\ \ \ }$

$14 \div 2 =$

$\begin{array}{r} 8 \\ \times\ 2 \\ \hline \end{array}$

$\begin{array}{r} 6 \\ \times\ 4 \\ \hline \end{array}$

$\begin{array}{r} 15 \\ +\ 3 \\ \hline \end{array}$

$\begin{array}{r} 3 \\ \times\ 3 \\ \hline \end{array}$

$\dfrac{5}{12} = \dfrac{\ \ \ }{36}$

$\dfrac{30}{5} =$

$\dfrac{7}{13} = \dfrac{21}{\ \ \ }$

$\dfrac{1}{7} = \dfrac{2}{\ \ \ }$

$24 \div 6 =$

$\begin{array}{r} 16 \\ -\ 7 \\ \hline \end{array}$

$\begin{array}{r} 7 \\ +\ 6 \\ \hline \end{array}$

$6\overline{)54}\ =$

$\begin{array}{r} 11 \\ -\ 2 \\ \hline \end{array}$

$\begin{array}{r} 3 \\ +\ 8 \\ \hline \end{array}$

$\dfrac{18}{9} =$

$\dfrac{9}{14} = \dfrac{27}{\ \ \ }$

$\begin{array}{r} 8 \\ -\ 5 \\ \hline \end{array}$

$2\overline{)8}\ =$

$\dfrac{\ \ \ }{3} = \dfrac{16}{24}$

$\begin{array}{r} 2 \\ +\ 4 \\ \hline \end{array}$

$\begin{array}{r} 1 \\ \times\ 1 \\ \hline \end{array}$

$\begin{array}{r} 5 \\ \times\ 3 \\ \hline \end{array}$

$\begin{array}{r} 12 \\ +\ 5 \\ \hline \end{array}$

$\begin{array}{r} 27 \\ -\ 4 \\ \hline \end{array}$

$\begin{array}{r} 7 \\ \times\ 5 \\ \hline \end{array}$

$\begin{array}{r} 15 \\ -\ 7 \\ \hline \end{array}$

$\dfrac{\ \ \ }{15} = \dfrac{8}{30}$

$\begin{array}{r} 6 \\ \times\ 7 \\ \hline \end{array}$

$\dfrac{30}{3} =$

$\dfrac{\ \ \ }{7} = \dfrac{4}{14}$

$7\overline{)35}\ =$

$\begin{array}{r} 7 \\ +\ 7 \\ \hline \end{array}$

$\dfrac{7}{8} = \dfrac{49}{\ \ \ }$

$\begin{array}{r} 18 \\ -\ 6 \\ \hline \end{array}$

$\begin{array}{r} 8 \\ \times\ 8 \\ \hline \end{array}$

$8 \div 8 =$

$\dfrac{\ \ \ }{\ \ \ } = \dfrac{14}{28}$

$\begin{array}{r} 4 \\ \times\ 4 \\ \hline \end{array}$

$\dfrac{5}{\phantom{5}} = \dfrac{25}{30}$

$18 \div 3 =$

$\begin{array}{r} 7 \\ \times\ 4 \\ \hline \end{array}$

$\begin{array}{r} 5 \\ \times\ 5 \\ \hline \end{array}$

$\begin{array}{r} 5 \\ +\ 8 \\ \hline \end{array}$

$\begin{array}{r} 9 \\ \times\ 0 \\ \hline \end{array}$

$\dfrac{7}{\phantom{7}} = \dfrac{14}{20}$

$\dfrac{20}{2} =$

$\dfrac{7}{12} = \dfrac{21}{\phantom{21}}$

$\dfrac{1}{3} = \dfrac{4}{\phantom{4}}$

$35 \div 7 =$

$\begin{array}{r} 21 \\ -\ 3 \\ \hline \end{array}$

$\begin{array}{r} 15 \\ +\ 4 \\ \hline \end{array}$

$3\overline{)24} =$

$\begin{array}{r} 12 \\ -\ 4 \\ \hline \end{array}$

$\begin{array}{r} 16 \\ +\ 1 \\ \hline \end{array}$

$\dfrac{32}{4} =$

$\dfrac{8}{13} = \dfrac{16}{\phantom{16}}$

$\begin{array}{r} 16 \\ -\ 2 \\ \hline \end{array}$

$6\overline{)42} =$

$\dfrac{3}{7} = \dfrac{24}{\phantom{24}}$

$\begin{array}{r} 4 \\ +\ 5 \\ \hline \end{array}$

$\begin{array}{r} 7 \\ \times\ 8 \\ \hline \end{array}$

$\begin{array}{r} 8 \\ \times\ 5 \\ \hline \end{array}$

$\begin{array}{r} 6 \\ +\ 5 \\ \hline \end{array}$

$\begin{array}{r} 12 \\ -\ 4 \\ \hline \end{array}$

$\begin{array}{r} 6 \\ \times\ 3 \\ \hline \end{array}$

$\begin{array}{r} 26 \\ -\ 5 \\ \hline \end{array}$

$\dfrac{9}{10} = \dfrac{27}{\phantom{27}}$

$\begin{array}{r} 9 \\ \times\ 7 \\ \hline \end{array}$

$\dfrac{42}{7} =$

$\dfrac{5}{11} = \dfrac{15}{\phantom{15}}$

$8\overline{)24} =$

$\begin{array}{r} 3 \\ +\ 3 \\ \hline \end{array}$

$\dfrac{3}{8} = \dfrac{15}{\phantom{15}}$

$\begin{array}{r} 24 \\ -12 \\ \hline \end{array}$

$\begin{array}{r} 9 \\ \times\ 9 \\ \hline \end{array}$

$48 \div 6 =$

$\dfrac{1}{5} = \dfrac{6}{\phantom{6}}$

$$\begin{array}{r} 9 \\ \times\ 6 \\ \hline \end{array}$$

$$\frac{3}{4} = \frac{21}{\rule{1.5em}{0.4pt}}$$

$$15 \div 5 =$$

$$\begin{array}{r} 7 \\ \times\ 2 \\ \hline \end{array}$$

$$\begin{array}{r} 6 \\ \times\ 5 \\ \hline \end{array}$$

$$\begin{array}{r} 14 \\ +\ 4 \\ \hline \end{array}$$

$$\begin{array}{r} 8 \\ \times\ 8 \\ \hline \end{array}$$

$$\frac{1}{5} = \frac{4}{\rule{1.5em}{0.4pt}}$$

$$\frac{40}{4} =$$

$$\frac{1}{12} = \frac{7}{\rule{1.5em}{0.4pt}}$$

$$\frac{8}{11} = \frac{16}{\rule{1.5em}{0.4pt}}$$

$$40 \div 5 =$$

$$\begin{array}{r} 31 \\ -\ 2 \\ \hline \end{array}$$

$$\begin{array}{r} 5 \\ +\ 6 \\ \hline \end{array}$$

$$2\overline{)16} =$$

$$\begin{array}{r} 23 \\ -\ 4 \\ \hline \end{array}$$

$$\begin{array}{r} 9 \\ +\ 9 \\ \hline \end{array}$$

$$\frac{14}{2} =$$

$$\frac{4}{\rule{1.5em}{0.4pt}} = \frac{16}{36}$$

$$\begin{array}{r} 27 \\ -\ 6 \\ \hline \end{array}$$

$$3\overline{)21} =$$

$$\frac{7}{9} = \frac{28}{\rule{1.5em}{0.4pt}}$$

$$\begin{array}{r} 17 \\ +\ 2 \\ \hline \end{array}$$

$$\begin{array}{r} 2 \\ \times\ 2 \\ \hline \end{array}$$

$$\begin{array}{r} 6 \\ \times\ 6 \\ \hline \end{array}$$

$$\begin{array}{r} 3 \\ +\ 6 \\ \hline \end{array}$$

$$\begin{array}{r} 14 \\ -\ 6 \\ \hline \end{array}$$

$$\begin{array}{r} 9 \\ \times\ 4 \\ \hline \end{array}$$

$$\begin{array}{r} 19 \\ -\ 7 \\ \hline \end{array}$$

$$\frac{1}{/} = \frac{5}{\rule{1.5em}{0.4pt}}$$

$$\begin{array}{r} 8 \\ \times\ 6 \\ \hline \end{array}$$

$$\frac{16}{8} =$$

$$\frac{6}{\rule{1.5em}{0.4pt}} = \frac{18}{33}$$

$$8\overline{)24} =$$

$$\begin{array}{r} 7 \\ +\ 8 \\ \hline \end{array}$$

$$\frac{4}{13} = \frac{12}{\rule{1.5em}{0.4pt}}$$

$$\begin{array}{r} 20 \\ -\ 9 \\ \hline \end{array}$$

$$\begin{array}{r} 8 \\ \times\ 3 \\ \hline \end{array}$$

$$21 \div 7 =$$

$$\frac{3}{11} = \frac{21}{\rule{1.5em}{0.4pt}}$$

$$\begin{array}{r} 2 \\ \times\ 2 \\ \hline \end{array}$$

$$\frac{3}{5} = \frac{}{20}$$

$$8 \div 1 =$$

$$\begin{array}{r} 9 \\ \times\ 8 \\ \hline \end{array}$$

$$\begin{array}{r} 5 \\ \times\ 5 \\ \hline \end{array}$$

$$\begin{array}{r} 7 \\ +\ 8 \\ \hline \end{array}$$

$$\begin{array}{r} 3 \\ \times\ 2 \\ \hline \end{array}$$

$$\frac{1}{4} = \frac{5}{}$$

$$\frac{30}{5} =$$

$$\frac{6}{7} = \frac{36}{}$$

$$\frac{1}{} = \frac{3}{30}$$

$$28 \div 4 =$$

$$\begin{array}{r} 17 \\ -\ 8 \\ \hline \end{array}$$

$$\begin{array}{r} 5 \\ +\ 6 \\ \hline \end{array}$$

$$7\overline{)56} =$$

$$\begin{array}{r} 13 \\ -\ 4 \\ \hline \end{array}$$

$$\begin{array}{r} 6 \\ +\ 6 \\ \hline \end{array}$$

$$\frac{45}{9} =$$

$$\frac{3}{7} = \frac{9}{}$$

$$\begin{array}{r} 17 \\ -\ 5 \\ \hline \end{array}$$

$$3\overline{)27} =$$

$$\frac{7}{15} = \frac{}{45}$$

$$\begin{array}{r} 13 \\ +\ 5 \\ \hline \end{array}$$

$$\begin{array}{r} 7 \\ \times\ 7 \\ \hline \end{array}$$

$$\begin{array}{r} 7 \\ \times\ 8 \\ \hline \end{array}$$

$$\begin{array}{r} 11 \\ +\ 2 \\ \hline \end{array}$$

$$\begin{array}{r} 6 \\ -\ 4 \\ \hline \end{array}$$

$$\begin{array}{r} 4 \\ \times\ 3 \\ \hline \end{array}$$

$$\begin{array}{r} 19 \\ -\ 3 \\ \hline \end{array}$$

$$\frac{8}{15} = \frac{16}{}$$

$$\begin{array}{r} 4 \\ \times\ 0 \\ \hline \end{array}$$

$$\frac{21}{3} =$$

$$\frac{8}{9} = \frac{}{72}$$

$$6\overline{)42} =$$

$$\begin{array}{r} 9 \\ +\ 3 \\ \hline \end{array}$$

$$\frac{5}{9} = \frac{15}{}$$

$$\begin{array}{r} 10 \\ -\ 6 \\ \hline \end{array}$$

$$\begin{array}{r} 9 \\ \times\ 5 \\ \hline \end{array}$$

$$25 \div 5 =$$

$$\frac{5}{6} = \frac{25}{}$$

$$\begin{array}{r} 3 \\ \times\ 6 \\ \hline \end{array}$$

$$\frac{}{9} = \frac{16}{36}$$

$$36 \div 6 =$$

$$\begin{array}{r} 9 \\ \times\ 3 \\ \hline \end{array}$$

$$\begin{array}{r} 1 \\ \times\ 1 \\ \hline \end{array}$$

$$\begin{array}{r} 9 \\ +\ 4 \\ \hline \end{array}$$

$$\begin{array}{r} 3 \\ \times\ 3 \\ \hline \end{array}$$

$$\frac{3}{4} = \frac{15}{}$$

$$\frac{40}{5} =$$

$$\frac{4}{5} = \frac{}{35}$$

$$\frac{8}{13} = \frac{16}{}$$

$$10 \div 2 =$$

$$\begin{array}{r} 16 \\ -\ 7 \\ \hline \end{array}$$

$$\begin{array}{r} 4 \\ +\ 4 \\ \hline \end{array}$$

$$2\overline{)10} =$$

$$\begin{array}{r} 21 \\ -\ 4 \\ \hline \end{array}$$

$$\begin{array}{r} 5 \\ +\ 7 \\ \hline \end{array}$$

$$\frac{4}{4} =$$

$$\frac{7}{12} = \frac{14}{}$$

$$\begin{array}{r} 25 \\ -\ 4 \\ \hline \end{array}$$

$$9\overline{)72} =$$

$$\frac{1}{8} = \frac{3}{}$$

$$\begin{array}{r} 15 \\ +\ 2 \\ \hline \end{array}$$

$$\begin{array}{r} 5 \\ \times\ 6 \\ \hline \end{array}$$

$$\begin{array}{r} 8 \\ \times\ 8 \\ \hline \end{array}$$

$$\begin{array}{r} 6 \\ +\ 7 \\ \hline \end{array}$$

$$\begin{array}{r} 16 \\ -\ 5 \\ \hline \end{array}$$

$$\begin{array}{r} 8 \\ \times\ 4 \\ \hline \end{array}$$

$$\begin{array}{r} 8 \\ -\ 3 \\ \hline \end{array}$$

$$\frac{3}{10} = \frac{18}{}$$

$$\begin{array}{r} 4 \\ \times\ 7 \\ \hline \end{array}$$

$$\frac{16}{8} =$$

$$\frac{7}{8} = \frac{21}{}$$

$$2\overline{)18} =$$

$$\begin{array}{r} 14 \\ +\ 3 \\ \hline \end{array}$$

$$\frac{9}{12} = \frac{}{36}$$

$$\begin{array}{r} 14 \\ -\ 6 \\ \hline \end{array}$$

$$\begin{array}{r} 7 \\ \times\ 3 \\ \hline \end{array}$$

$$18 \div 6 =$$

$$\frac{1}{6} = \frac{5}{}$$

$\begin{array}{r} 2 \\ \times\ 4 \\ \hline \end{array}$   $\dfrac{5}{12} = \dfrac{10}{\phantom{xx}}$   $6 \div 3 =$   $\begin{array}{r} 8 \\ \times\ 5 \\ \hline \end{array}$   $\begin{array}{r} 7 \\ \times\ 7 \\ \hline \end{array}$

$\begin{array}{r} 8 \\ +\ 8 \\ \hline \end{array}$   $\begin{array}{r} 5 \\ \times\ 3 \\ \hline \end{array}$   $\dfrac{6}{15} = \dfrac{\phantom{xx}}{5}$   $\dfrac{15}{3} =$   $\dfrac{1}{8} = \dfrac{4}{\phantom{xx}}$

$\dfrac{\phantom{xx}}{9} = \dfrac{4}{18}$   $8 \div 8 =$   $\begin{array}{r} 17 \\ -\ 2 \\ \hline \end{array}$   $\begin{array}{r} 9 \\ +\ 4 \\ \hline \end{array}$   $2\overline{)14} =$

$\begin{array}{r} 25 \\ -\ 6 \\ \hline \end{array}$   $\begin{array}{r} 13 \\ +\ 6 \\ \hline \end{array}$   $\dfrac{81}{9} =$   $\dfrac{1}{2} = \dfrac{7}{\phantom{xx}}$   $\begin{array}{r} 22 \\ -\ 4 \\ \hline \end{array}$

$7\overline{)35} =$   $\dfrac{8}{11} = \dfrac{24}{\phantom{xx}}$   $\begin{array}{r} 7 \\ +\ 5 \\ \hline \end{array}$   $\begin{array}{r} 12 \\ \times 12 \\ \hline \end{array}$   $\begin{array}{r} 4 \\ \times\ 6 \\ \hline \end{array}$

$\begin{array}{r} 17 \\ +\ 3 \\ \hline \end{array}$   $\begin{array}{r} 9 \\ -\ 4 \\ \hline \end{array}$   $\begin{array}{r} 3 \\ \times\ 3 \\ \hline \end{array}$   $\begin{array}{r} 16 \\ -\ 9 \\ \hline \end{array}$   $\dfrac{2}{7} = \dfrac{\phantom{xx}}{42}$

$\begin{array}{r} 7 \\ \times\ 4 \\ \hline \end{array}$   $\dfrac{24}{3} =$   $\dfrac{5}{8} = \dfrac{15}{\phantom{xx}}$   $6\overline{)42} =$   $\begin{array}{r} 6 \\ +\ 7 \\ \hline \end{array}$

$\dfrac{6}{11} = \dfrac{18}{\phantom{xx}}$   $\begin{array}{r} 18 \\ -\ 5 \\ \hline \end{array}$   $\begin{array}{r} 6 \\ \times\ 9 \\ \hline \end{array}$   $40 \div 5 =$   $\dfrac{8}{15} = \dfrac{\phantom{xx}}{30}$

$$\begin{array}{r} 10 \\ \times\ 10 \\ \hline \end{array}$$

$$\frac{1}{3} = \frac{6}{\phantom{x}}$$

$$30 \div 6 =$$

$$\begin{array}{r} 4 \\ \times\ 4 \\ \hline \end{array}$$

$$\begin{array}{r} 7 \\ \times\ 3 \\ \hline \end{array}$$

$$\begin{array}{r} 13 \\ +\ 7 \\ \hline \end{array}$$

$$\begin{array}{r} 6 \\ \times\ 7 \\ \hline \end{array}$$

$$\frac{3}{5} = \frac{\phantom{x}}{30}$$

$$\frac{35}{5} =$$

$$\frac{4}{13} = \frac{8}{\phantom{x}}$$

$$\frac{4}{7} = \frac{16}{\phantom{x}}$$

$$18 \div 3 =$$

$$\begin{array}{r} 23 \\ -\ 5 \\ \hline \end{array}$$

$$\begin{array}{r} 18 \\ +\ 2 \\ \hline \end{array}$$

$$1\overline{)5} =$$

$$\begin{array}{r} 15 \\ -\ 8 \\ \hline \end{array}$$

$$\begin{array}{r} 9 \\ +\ 9 \\ \hline \end{array}$$

$$\frac{6}{2} =$$

$$\frac{2}{7} = \frac{\phantom{x}}{35}$$

$$\begin{array}{r} 20 \\ -\ 10 \\ \hline \end{array}$$

$$6\overline{)24} =$$

$$\frac{\phantom{x}}{10} = \frac{7}{70}$$

$$\begin{array}{r} 8 \\ +\ 9 \\ \hline \end{array}$$

$$\begin{array}{r} 8 \\ \times\ 2 \\ \hline \end{array}$$

$$\begin{array}{r} 9 \\ \times\ 4 \\ \hline \end{array}$$

$$\begin{array}{r} 7 \\ +\ 8 \\ \hline \end{array}$$

$$\begin{array}{r} 16 \\ -\ 3 \\ \hline \end{array}$$

$$\begin{array}{r} 3 \\ \times\ 3 \\ \hline \end{array}$$

$$\begin{array}{r} 14 \\ -\ 3 \\ \hline \end{array}$$

$$\frac{7}{10} = \frac{28}{\phantom{x}}$$

$$\begin{array}{r} 9 \\ \times\ 0 \\ \hline \end{array}$$

$$\frac{49}{7} =$$

$$\frac{7}{9} = \frac{21}{\phantom{x}}$$

$$9\overline{)63} =$$

$$\begin{array}{r} 5 \\ +\ 5 \\ \hline \end{array}$$

$$\frac{9}{11} = \frac{54}{\phantom{x}}$$

$$\begin{array}{r} 15 \\ -\ 8 \\ \hline \end{array}$$

$$\begin{array}{r} 0 \\ \times\ 8 \\ \hline \end{array}$$

$$16 \div 8 =$$

$$\frac{9}{10} = \frac{\phantom{x}}{40}$$

Name:_____

$$\begin{array}{r} 3 \\ \times\ 5 \\ \hline \end{array}$$

$$\frac{1}{7} = \frac{}{63}$$

$$27 \div 9 =$$

$$\begin{array}{r} 6 \\ \times\ 6 \\ \hline \end{array}$$

$$\begin{array}{r} 1 \\ \times\ 1 \\ \hline \end{array}$$

$$\begin{array}{r} 7 \\ +\ 7 \\ \hline \end{array}$$

$$\begin{array}{r} 7 \\ \times\ 6 \\ \hline \end{array}$$

$$\frac{6}{11} = \frac{18}{}$$

$$\frac{30}{3} =$$

$$\frac{5}{6} = \frac{15}{}$$

$$\frac{8}{15} = \frac{24}{}$$

$$24 \div 6 =$$

$$\begin{array}{r} 19 \\ -\ 7 \\ \hline \end{array}$$

$$\begin{array}{r} 16 \\ +\ 1 \\ \hline \end{array}$$

$$8\overline{)24} =$$

$$\begin{array}{r} 22 \\ -\ 11 \\ \hline \end{array}$$

$$\begin{array}{r} 4 \\ +\ 6 \\ \hline \end{array}$$

$$\frac{42}{7} =$$

$$\frac{4}{9} = \frac{16}{}$$

$$\begin{array}{r} 23 \\ -\ 4 \\ \hline \end{array}$$

$$6\overline{)48} =$$

$$\frac{1}{5} = \frac{}{25}$$

$$\begin{array}{r} 7 \\ +\ 8 \\ \hline \end{array}$$

$$\begin{array}{r} 9 \\ \times\ 3 \\ \hline \end{array}$$

$$\begin{array}{r} 6 \\ \times\ 2 \\ \hline \end{array}$$

$$\begin{array}{r} 11 \\ +\ 3 \\ \hline \end{array}$$

$$\begin{array}{r} 14 \\ -\ 6 \\ \hline \end{array}$$

$$\begin{array}{r} 6 \\ \times\ 4 \\ \hline \end{array}$$

$$\begin{array}{r} 17 \\ -\ 3 \\ \hline \end{array}$$

$$\frac{3}{5} = \frac{9}{}$$

$$\begin{array}{r} 4 \\ \times\ 9 \\ \hline \end{array}$$

$$\frac{32}{4} =$$

$$\frac{7}{9} = \frac{}{63}$$

$$2\overline{)8} =$$

$$\begin{array}{r} 9 \\ +\ 9 \\ \hline \end{array}$$

$$\frac{9}{11} = \frac{36}{}$$

$$\begin{array}{r} 11 \\ -\ 2 \\ \hline \end{array}$$

$$\begin{array}{r} 4 \\ \times\ 4 \\ \hline \end{array}$$

$$14 \div 2 =$$

$$\frac{2}{11} = \frac{}{33}$$

$$4 \times 4$$

$$\frac{8}{9} = \frac{72}{\phantom{0}}$$

$$35 \div 7 =$$

$$5 \times 3$$

$$8 \times 7$$

$$5 + 7$$

$$5 \times 8$$

$$\frac{2}{3} = \frac{16}{\phantom{0}}$$

$$\frac{18}{6} =$$

$$\frac{7}{9} = \frac{56}{\phantom{0}}$$

$$\frac{1}{3} = \frac{6}{\phantom{0}}$$

$$21 \div 3 =$$

$$19 - 6$$

$$14 + 14$$

$$6\overline{)54} =$$

$$12 - 3$$

$$13 + 5$$

$$\frac{9}{3} =$$

$$\frac{4}{15} = \frac{\phantom{0}}{45}$$

$$8 - 5$$

$$3\overline{)24} =$$

$$\frac{9}{11} = \frac{27}{\phantom{0}}$$

$$11 + 4$$

$$7 \times 7$$

$$9 \times 6$$

$$9 + 3$$

$$17 - 8$$

$$11 \times 11$$

$$34 - 3$$

$$\frac{5}{8} = \frac{25}{\phantom{0}}$$

$$3 \times 4$$

$$\frac{81}{9} =$$

$$\frac{1}{9} = \frac{9}{\phantom{0}}$$

$$7\overline{)28} =$$

$$2 + 2$$

$$\frac{3}{4} = \frac{\phantom{0}}{12}$$

$$12 - 7$$

$$7 \times 4$$

$$48 \div 6 =$$

$$\frac{6}{11} = \frac{36}{\phantom{0}}$$

$$\begin{array}{r} 6 \\ \times\ 6 \\ \hline \end{array}$$

$$\frac{2}{9} = \frac{}{36}$$

$$18 \div 6 =$$

$$\begin{array}{r} 6 \\ \times\ 3 \\ \hline \end{array}$$

$$\begin{array}{r} 5 \\ \times\ 4 \\ \hline \end{array}$$

$$\begin{array}{r} 2 \\ +\ 3 \\ \hline \end{array}$$

$$\begin{array}{r} 9 \\ \times\ 7 \\ \hline \end{array}$$

$$\frac{5}{11} = \frac{35}{}$$

$$\frac{16}{8} =$$

$$\frac{4}{9} = \frac{16}{}$$

$$\frac{8}{9} = \frac{}{81}$$

$$14 \div 7 =$$

$$\begin{array}{r} 13 \\ -\ 5 \\ \hline \end{array}$$

$$\begin{array}{r} 13 \\ +\ 4 \\ \hline \end{array}$$

$$6\overline{)24} =$$

$$\begin{array}{r} 6 \\ -\ 3 \\ \hline \end{array}$$

$$\begin{array}{r} 8 \\ +\ 9 \\ \hline \end{array}$$

$$\frac{45}{5} =$$

$$\frac{6}{13} = \frac{18}{}$$

$$\begin{array}{r} 16 \\ -\ 2 \\ \hline \end{array}$$

$$3\overline{)9} =$$

$$\frac{3}{7} = \frac{21}{}$$

$$\begin{array}{r} 4 \\ +\ 8 \\ \hline \end{array}$$

$$\begin{array}{r} 5 \\ \times\ 2 \\ \hline \end{array}$$

$$\begin{array}{r} 5 \\ \times\ 5 \\ \hline \end{array}$$

$$\begin{array}{r} 8 \\ +\ 6 \\ \hline \end{array}$$

$$\begin{array}{r} 17 \\ -\ 4 \\ \hline \end{array}$$

$$\begin{array}{r} 7 \\ \times\ 5 \\ \hline \end{array}$$

$$\begin{array}{r} 10 \\ -\ 5 \\ \hline \end{array}$$

$$\frac{7}{10} = \frac{42}{}$$

$$\begin{array}{r} 9 \\ \times\ 9 \\ \hline \end{array}$$

$$\frac{4}{2} =$$

$$\frac{1}{12} = \frac{5}{}$$

$$7\overline{)49} =$$

$$\begin{array}{r} 12 \\ +\ 5 \\ \hline \end{array}$$

$$\frac{9}{14} = \frac{18}{}$$

$$\begin{array}{r} 16 \\ -\ 7 \\ \hline \end{array}$$

$$\begin{array}{r} 8 \\ \times\ 9 \\ \hline \end{array}$$

$$15 \div 3 =$$

$$\frac{1}{6} = \frac{7}{}$$

$$\begin{array}{r} 8 \\ \times\ 8 \\ \hline \end{array}$$

$$\frac{4}{5} = \frac{20}{\phantom{0}}$$

$$12 \div 3 =$$

$$\begin{array}{r} 5 \\ \times\ 7 \\ \hline \end{array}$$

$$\begin{array}{r} 7 \\ \times\ 9 \\ \hline \end{array}$$

$$\begin{array}{r} 3 \\ +\ 9 \\ \hline \end{array}$$

$$\begin{array}{r} 9 \\ \times\ 4 \\ \hline \end{array}$$

$$\frac{1}{\phantom{0}} = \frac{2}{12}$$

$$\frac{12}{2} =$$

$$\frac{7}{10} = \frac{63}{\phantom{0}}$$

$$\frac{1}{4} = \frac{6}{\phantom{0}}$$

$$35 \div 5 =$$

$$\begin{array}{r} 23 \\ -\ 2 \\ \hline \end{array}$$

$$\begin{array}{r} 5 \\ +\ 5 \\ \hline \end{array}$$

$$3\overline{)21} \ =$$

$$\begin{array}{r} 11 \\ -\ 3 \\ \hline \end{array}$$

$$\begin{array}{r} 12 \\ +\ 3 \\ \hline \end{array}$$

$$\frac{30}{5} =$$

$$\frac{\phantom{0}}{10} = \frac{6}{20}$$

$$\begin{array}{r} 16 \\ -\ 8 \\ \hline \end{array}$$

$$4\overline{)28} \ =$$

$$\frac{5}{12} = \frac{30}{\phantom{0}}$$

$$\begin{array}{r} 11 \\ +\ 2 \\ \hline \end{array}$$

$$\begin{array}{r} 8 \\ \times\ 3 \\ \hline \end{array}$$

$$\begin{array}{r} 9 \\ \times\ 9 \\ \hline \end{array}$$

$$\begin{array}{r} 6 \\ +\ 6 \\ \hline \end{array}$$

$$\begin{array}{r} 12 \\ -\ 5 \\ \hline \end{array}$$

$$\begin{array}{r} 6 \\ \times\ 6 \\ \hline \end{array}$$

$$\begin{array}{r} 19 \\ -\ 5 \\ \hline \end{array}$$

$$\frac{6}{11} = \frac{18}{\phantom{0}}$$

$$\begin{array}{r} 4 \\ \times\ 5 \\ \hline \end{array}$$

$$\frac{20}{2} =$$

$$\frac{2}{7} = \frac{\phantom{0}}{21}$$

$$6\overline{)54} \ =$$

$$\begin{array}{r} 7 \\ +\ 9 \\ \hline \end{array}$$

$$\frac{8}{15} = \frac{\phantom{0}}{30}$$

$$\begin{array}{r} 16 \\ -\ 9 \\ \hline \end{array}$$

$$\begin{array}{r} 7 \\ \times\ 0 \\ \hline \end{array}$$

$$18 \div 3 =$$

$$\frac{9}{12} = \frac{\phantom{0}}{4}$$

$$\begin{array}{r} 3 \\ \times\ 6 \\ \hline \end{array}$$

$$\frac{1}{6} = \frac{}{36}$$

$6 \div 3 =$

$$\begin{array}{r} 7 \\ \times\ 4 \\ \hline \end{array}$$

$$\begin{array}{r} 8 \\ \times\ 8 \\ \hline \end{array}$$

$$\begin{array}{r} 5 \\ +\ 5 \\ \hline \end{array}$$

$$\begin{array}{r} 5 \\ \times\ 7 \\ \hline \end{array}$$

$$\frac{6}{7} = \frac{30}{}$$

$$\frac{32}{4} =$$

$$\frac{2}{9} = \frac{6}{}$$

$$\frac{9}{10} = \frac{81}{}$$

$14 \div 7 =$

$$\begin{array}{r} 15 \\ -\ 6 \\ \hline \end{array}$$

$$\begin{array}{r} 13 \\ +\ 5 \\ \hline \end{array}$$

$5\overline{)30} =$

$$\begin{array}{r} 8 \\ -\ 4 \\ \hline \end{array}$$

$$\begin{array}{r} 3 \\ +\ 5 \\ \hline \end{array}$$

$$\frac{20}{2} =$$

$$\frac{5}{12} = \frac{30}{}$$

$$\begin{array}{r} 21 \\ -\ 2 \\ \hline \end{array}$$

$7\overline{)56} =$

$$\frac{8}{9} = \frac{}{72}$$

$$\begin{array}{r} 7 \\ +\ 8 \\ \hline \end{array}$$

$$\begin{array}{r} 6 \\ \times\ 6 \\ \hline \end{array}$$

$$\begin{array}{r} 3 \\ \times\ 3 \\ \hline \end{array}$$

$$\begin{array}{r} 8 \\ +\ 8 \\ \hline \end{array}$$

$$\begin{array}{r} 4 \\ -\ 2 \\ \hline \end{array}$$

$$\begin{array}{r} 6 \\ \times\ 2 \\ \hline \end{array}$$

$$\begin{array}{r} 15 \\ -\ 4 \\ \hline \end{array}$$

$$\frac{3}{10} = \frac{9}{}$$

$$\begin{array}{r} 9 \\ \times\ 8 \\ \hline \end{array}$$

$$\frac{16}{8} =$$

$$\frac{4}{11} = \frac{16}{}$$

$3\overline{)24} =$

$$\begin{array}{r} 17 \\ +\ 3 \\ \hline \end{array}$$

$$\frac{7}{8} = \frac{56}{}$$

$$\begin{array}{r} 18 \\ -\ 3 \\ \hline \end{array}$$

$$\begin{array}{r} 5 \\ \times\ 3 \\ \hline \end{array}$$

$24 \div 6 =$

$$\frac{1}{5} = \frac{}{25}$$

$\begin{array}{r} 4 \\ \times\ 4 \\ \hline \end{array}$    $\dfrac{2}{3} = \dfrac{18}{\phantom{00}}$    $25 \div 5 =$    $\begin{array}{r} 4 \\ \times\ 5 \\ \hline \end{array}$    $\begin{array}{r} 6 \\ \times\ 8 \\ \hline \end{array}$

$\begin{array}{r} 9 \\ +\ 7 \\ \hline \end{array}$    $\begin{array}{r} 10 \\ \times\ 10 \\ \hline \end{array}$    $\dfrac{3}{7} = \dfrac{18}{\phantom{00}}$    $\dfrac{64}{8} =$    $\dfrac{6}{17} = \dfrac{\phantom{00}}{34}$

$\dfrac{1}{5} = \dfrac{5}{\phantom{00}}$    $15 \div 3 =$    $\begin{array}{r} 18 \\ -\ 6 \\ \hline \end{array}$    $\begin{array}{r} 17 \\ +\ 1 \\ \hline \end{array}$    $6\overline{)24}\ =$

$\begin{array}{r} 10 \\ -\ 2 \\ \hline \end{array}$    $\begin{array}{r} 3 \\ +\ 4 \\ \hline \end{array}$    $\dfrac{45}{5} =$    $\dfrac{4}{7} = \dfrac{16}{\phantom{00}}$    $\begin{array}{r} 15 \\ -\ 7 \\ \hline \end{array}$

$3\overline{)9}\ =$    $\dfrac{5}{6} = \dfrac{20}{\phantom{00}}$    $\begin{array}{r} 7 \\ +\ 4 \\ \hline \end{array}$    $\begin{array}{r} 5 \\ \times\ 6 \\ \hline \end{array}$    $\begin{array}{r} 7 \\ \times\ 7 \\ \hline \end{array}$

$\begin{array}{r} 8 \\ +\ 8 \\ \hline \end{array}$    $\begin{array}{r} 14 \\ -\ 5 \\ \hline \end{array}$    $\begin{array}{r} 3 \\ \times\ 4 \\ \hline \end{array}$    $\begin{array}{r} 18 \\ -\ 9 \\ \hline \end{array}$    $\dfrac{9}{11} = \dfrac{81}{\phantom{00}}$

$\begin{array}{r} 4 \\ \times\ 0 \\ \hline \end{array}$    $\dfrac{4}{2} =$    $\dfrac{7}{8} = \dfrac{14}{\phantom{00}}$    $7\overline{)63}\ =$    $\begin{array}{r} 16 \\ +\ 3 \\ \hline \end{array}$

$\dfrac{1}{8} = \dfrac{6}{\phantom{00}}$    $\begin{array}{r} 27 \\ -\ 4 \\ \hline \end{array}$    $\begin{array}{r} 3 \\ \times\ 7 \\ \hline \end{array}$    $36 \div 4 =$    $\dfrac{8}{15} = \dfrac{\phantom{00}}{45}$

$$\begin{array}{r} 12 \\ \times\ 12 \\ \hline \end{array}$$

$$\frac{1}{3} = \frac{10}{}$$

$$36 \div 6 =$$

$$\begin{array}{r} 9 \\ \times\ 6 \\ \hline \end{array}$$

$$\begin{array}{r} 4 \\ \times\ 3 \\ \hline \end{array}$$

$$\begin{array}{r} 5 \\ +\ 7 \\ \hline \end{array}$$

$$\begin{array}{r} 7 \\ \times\ 7 \\ \hline \end{array}$$

$$\frac{9}{10} = \frac{27}{}$$

$$\frac{14}{2} =$$

$$\frac{4}{5} = \frac{16}{}$$

$$\frac{8}{11} = \frac{64}{}$$

$$72 \div 8 =$$

$$\begin{array}{r} 27 \\ -\ 5 \\ \hline \end{array}$$

$$\begin{array}{r} 11 \\ +\ 6 \\ \hline \end{array}$$

$$6\overline{)24} =$$

$$\begin{array}{r} 14 \\ -\ 7 \\ \hline \end{array}$$

$$\begin{array}{r} 5 \\ +\ 8 \\ \hline \end{array}$$

$$\frac{15}{5} =$$

$$\frac{5}{11} = \frac{25}{}$$

$$\begin{array}{r} 22 \\ -\ 3 \\ \hline \end{array}$$

$$3\overline{)27} =$$

$$\frac{1}{10} = \frac{3}{}$$

$$\begin{array}{r} 10 \\ +\ 10 \\ \hline \end{array}$$

$$\begin{array}{r} 7 \\ \times\ 8 \\ \hline \end{array}$$

$$\begin{array}{r} 5 \\ \times\ 4 \\ \hline \end{array}$$

$$\begin{array}{r} 6 \\ +\ 9 \\ \hline \end{array}$$

$$\begin{array}{r} 9 \\ -\ 5 \\ \hline \end{array}$$

$$\begin{array}{r} 9 \\ \times\ 3 \\ \hline \end{array}$$

$$\begin{array}{r} 11 \\ -\ 4 \\ \hline \end{array}$$

$$\frac{3}{4} = \frac{15}{}$$

$$\begin{array}{r} 8 \\ \times\ 5 \\ \hline \end{array}$$

$$\frac{32}{8} =$$

$$\frac{7}{8} = \frac{49}{}$$

$$2\overline{)18} =$$

$$\begin{array}{r} 17 \\ +\ 4 \\ \hline \end{array}$$

$$\frac{6}{7} = \frac{36}{}$$

$$\begin{array}{r} 24 \\ -\ 3 \\ \hline \end{array}$$

$$\begin{array}{r} 1 \\ \times\ 1 \\ \hline \end{array}$$

$$18 \div 6 =$$

$$\frac{2}{7} = \frac{14}{}$$

$$\begin{array}{r} 3 \\ \times\ 3 \\ \hline \end{array}$$

$$\frac{8}{9}=\frac{}{81}$$

$$27 \div 9 =$$

$$\begin{array}{r} 9 \\ \times\ 4 \\ \hline \end{array}$$

$$\begin{array}{r} 4 \\ \times\ 6 \\ \hline \end{array}$$

$$\begin{array}{r} 7 \\ +\ 8 \\ \hline \end{array}$$

$$\begin{array}{r} 5 \\ \times\ 2 \\ \hline \end{array}$$

$$\frac{3}{8}=\frac{24}{}$$

$$\frac{49}{7}=$$

$$\frac{5}{7}=\frac{}{42}$$

$$\frac{1}{8}=\frac{4}{}$$

$$35 \div 5 =$$

$$\begin{array}{r} 16 \\ -\ 4 \\ \hline \end{array}$$

$$\begin{array}{r} 9 \\ +\ 7 \\ \hline \end{array}$$

$$9\overline{)72} =$$

$$\begin{array}{r} 13 \\ -\ 6 \\ \hline \end{array}$$

$$\begin{array}{r} 14 \\ +\ 5 \\ \hline \end{array}$$

$$\frac{40}{5}=$$

$$\frac{1}{12}=\frac{4}{}$$

$$\begin{array}{r} 17 \\ -\ 6 \\ \hline \end{array}$$

$$2\overline{)14} =$$

$$\frac{9}{10}=\frac{}{40}$$

$$\begin{array}{r} 15 \\ +\ 2 \\ \hline \end{array}$$

$$\begin{array}{r} 8 \\ \times\ 8 \\ \hline \end{array}$$

$$\begin{array}{r} 3 \\ \times\ 5 \\ \hline \end{array}$$

$$\begin{array}{r} 5 \\ +\ 9 \\ \hline \end{array}$$

$$\begin{array}{r} 16 \\ -\ 7 \\ \hline \end{array}$$

$$\begin{array}{r} 8 \\ \times\ 3 \\ \hline \end{array}$$

$$\begin{array}{r} 12 \\ -\ 6 \\ \hline \end{array}$$

$$\frac{6}{7}=\frac{36}{}$$

$$\begin{array}{r} 7 \\ \times\ 9 \\ \hline \end{array}$$

$$\frac{21}{3}=$$

$$\frac{4}{5}=\frac{}{20}$$

$$6\overline{)54} =$$

$$\begin{array}{r} 6 \\ +\ 8 \\ \hline \end{array}$$

$$\frac{2}{7}=\frac{8}{}$$

$$\begin{array}{r} 14 \\ -\ 8 \\ \hline \end{array}$$

$$\begin{array}{r} 5 \\ \times\ 5 \\ \hline \end{array}$$

$$10 \div 2 =$$

$$\frac{7}{12}=\frac{21}{}$$

$\begin{array}{r} 4 \\ \times\ 7 \\ \hline \end{array}$

$\dfrac{4}{9} = \dfrac{20}{\phantom{0}}$

$20 \div 4 =$

$\begin{array}{r} 8 \\ \times\ 0 \\ \hline \end{array}$

$\begin{array}{r} 9 \\ \times\ 9 \\ \hline \end{array}$

$\begin{array}{r} 3 \\ +\ 3 \\ \hline \end{array}$

$\begin{array}{r} 8 \\ \times\ 8 \\ \hline \end{array}$

$\dfrac{2}{5} = \dfrac{\phantom{0}}{50}$

$\dfrac{30}{5} =$

$\dfrac{6}{11} = \dfrac{36}{\phantom{0}}$

$\dfrac{\phantom{0}}{\phantom{0}} = \dfrac{14}{28}$

$14 \div 2 =$

$\begin{array}{r} 20 \\ -\ 10 \\ \hline \end{array}$

$\begin{array}{r} 15 \\ +\ 3 \\ \hline \end{array}$

$6\overline{)54} =$

$\begin{array}{r} 16 \\ -\ 7 \\ \hline \end{array}$

$\begin{array}{r} 3 \\ +\ 8 \\ \hline \end{array}$

$\dfrac{12}{2} =$

$\dfrac{7}{9} = \dfrac{49}{\phantom{0}}$

$\begin{array}{r} 16 \\ -\ 3 \\ \hline \end{array}$

$8\overline{)24} =$

$\dfrac{\phantom{0}}{\phantom{0}} = \dfrac{5}{50}$

$\begin{array}{r} 9 \\ +\ 9 \\ \hline \end{array}$

$\begin{array}{r} 8 \\ \times\ 3 \\ \hline \end{array}$

$\begin{array}{r} 7 \\ \times\ 2 \\ \hline \end{array}$

$\begin{array}{r} 9 \\ +\ 2 \\ \hline \end{array}$

$\begin{array}{r} 21 \\ -\ 3 \\ \hline \end{array}$

$\begin{array}{r} 8 \\ \times\ 7 \\ \hline \end{array}$

$\begin{array}{r} 17 \\ -\ 5 \\ \hline \end{array}$

$\dfrac{8}{13} = \dfrac{24}{\phantom{0}}$

$\begin{array}{r} 5 \\ \times\ 9 \\ \hline \end{array}$

$\dfrac{40}{8} =$

$\dfrac{5}{12} = \dfrac{20}{\phantom{0}}$

$3\overline{)21} =$

$\begin{array}{r} 12 \\ +\ 6 \\ \hline \end{array}$

$\dfrac{3}{8} = \dfrac{\phantom{0}}{40}$

$\begin{array}{r} 13 \\ -\ 4 \\ \hline \end{array}$

$\begin{array}{r} 5 \\ \times\ 5 \\ \hline \end{array}$

$40 \div 5 =$

$\dfrac{9}{12} = \dfrac{\phantom{0}}{\phantom{0}}$

Name: _____

$$\begin{array}{r} 9 \\ \times\ 9 \\ \hline \end{array}$$

$$\frac{8}{11} = \frac{64}{}$$

$$21 \div 3 =$$

$$\begin{array}{r} 6 \\ \times\ 6 \\ \hline \end{array}$$

$$\begin{array}{r} 7 \\ \times\ 8 \\ \hline \end{array}$$

$$\begin{array}{r} 8 \\ +\ 3 \\ \hline \end{array}$$

$$\begin{array}{r} 6 \\ \times\ 7 \\ \hline \end{array}$$

$$\frac{3}{} = \frac{9}{15}$$

$$\frac{81}{9} =$$

$$\frac{4}{7} = \frac{}{28}$$

$$\frac{}{} = \frac{15}{30}$$

$$15 \div 5 =$$

$$\begin{array}{r} 19 \\ -\ 3 \\ \hline \end{array}$$

$$\begin{array}{r} 14 \\ +\ 3 \\ \hline \end{array}$$

$$1\overline{)5} =$$

$$\begin{array}{r} 15 \\ -\ 8 \\ \hline \end{array}$$

$$\begin{array}{r} 17 \\ +\ 2 \\ \hline \end{array}$$

$$\frac{24}{3} =$$

$$\frac{}{} = \frac{12}{18}$$

$$\begin{array}{r} 15 \\ -\ 8 \\ \hline \end{array}$$

$$6\overline{)48} =$$

$$\frac{5}{} = \frac{15}{33}$$

$$\begin{array}{r} 6 \\ +\ 7 \\ \hline \end{array}$$

$$\begin{array}{r} 9 \\ \times\ 5 \\ \hline \end{array}$$

$$\begin{array}{r} 6 \\ \times\ 4 \\ \hline \end{array}$$

$$\begin{array}{r} 5 \\ +\ 6 \\ \hline \end{array}$$

$$\begin{array}{r} 21 \\ -\ 4 \\ \hline \end{array}$$

$$\begin{array}{r} 11 \\ \times 11 \\ \hline \end{array}$$

$$\begin{array}{r} 14 \\ -\ 2 \\ \hline \end{array}$$

$$\frac{}{10} = \frac{49}{70}$$

$$\begin{array}{r} 3 \\ \times\ 2 \\ \hline \end{array}$$

$$\frac{4}{4} =$$

$$\frac{}{} = \frac{5}{40}$$

$$7\overline{)49} =$$

$$\begin{array}{r} 8 \\ +\ 9 \\ \hline \end{array}$$

$$\frac{}{12} = \frac{27}{36}$$

$$\begin{array}{r} 6 \\ -\ 4 \\ \hline \end{array}$$

$$\begin{array}{r} 5 \\ \times\ 3 \\ \hline \end{array}$$

$$16 \div 8 =$$

$$\frac{6}{} = \frac{42}{49}$$

$$\begin{array}{r} 2 \\ \times\ 2 \\ \hline \end{array}$$

$$\frac{5}{6} = \frac{10}{\phantom{0}}$$

$$28 \div 4 =$$

$$\begin{array}{r} 8 \\ \times\ 6 \\ \hline \end{array}$$

$$\begin{array}{r} 7 \\ \times\ 0 \\ \hline \end{array}$$

$$\begin{array}{r} 2 \\ +\ 4 \\ \hline \end{array}$$

$$\begin{array}{r} 2 \\ \times\ 4 \\ \hline \end{array}$$

$$\frac{7}{15} = \frac{21}{\phantom{0}}$$

$$\frac{30}{3} =$$

$$\frac{2}{\phantom{0}} = \frac{4}{18}$$

$$\frac{9}{14} = \frac{18}{\phantom{0}}$$

$$21 \div 7 =$$

$$\begin{array}{r} 13 \\ -\ 6 \\ \hline \end{array}$$

$$\begin{array}{r} 4 \\ +\ 5 \\ \hline \end{array}$$

$$2\overline{)8} =$$

$$\begin{array}{r} 7 \\ -\ 4 \\ \hline \end{array}$$

$$\begin{array}{r} 9 \\ +\ 3 \\ \hline \end{array}$$

$$\frac{18}{6} =$$

$$\frac{6}{9} = \frac{2}{\phantom{0}}$$

$$\begin{array}{r} 17 \\ -\ 2 \\ \hline \end{array}$$

$$9\overline{)63} =$$

$$\frac{3}{5} = \frac{12}{\phantom{0}}$$

$$\begin{array}{r} 13 \\ +\ 6 \\ \hline \end{array}$$

$$\begin{array}{r} 7 \\ \times\ 5 \\ \hline \end{array}$$

$$\begin{array}{r} 4 \\ \times\ 9 \\ \hline \end{array}$$

$$\begin{array}{r} 6 \\ +\ 7 \\ \hline \end{array}$$

$$\begin{array}{r} 22 \\ -\ 4 \\ \hline \end{array}$$

$$\begin{array}{r} 9 \\ \times\ 3 \\ \hline \end{array}$$

$$\begin{array}{r} 26 \\ -\ 5 \\ \hline \end{array}$$

$$\frac{1}{4} = \frac{6}{\phantom{0}}$$

$$\begin{array}{r} 6 \\ \times\ 6 \\ \hline \end{array}$$

$$\frac{45}{9} =$$

$$\frac{8}{13} = \frac{\phantom{0}}{26}$$

$$6\overline{)42} =$$

$$\begin{array}{r} 15 \\ +\ 4 \\ \hline \end{array}$$

$$\frac{4}{13} = \frac{\phantom{0}}{26}$$

$$\begin{array}{r} 12 \\ -\ 4 \\ \hline \end{array}$$

$$\begin{array}{r} 4 \\ \times\ 4 \\ \hline \end{array}$$

$$18 \div 3 =$$

$$\frac{1}{7} = \frac{3}{\phantom{0}}$$

$$\begin{array}{r} 2 \\ \times\ 2 \\ \hline \end{array}$$

$$— = \frac{16}{32}$$

$$21 \div 3 =$$

$$\begin{array}{r} 7 \\ \times\ 3 \\ \hline \end{array}$$

$$\begin{array}{r} 3 \\ \times\ 3 \\ \hline \end{array}$$

$$\begin{array}{r} 4 \\ +\ 9 \\ \hline \end{array}$$

$$\begin{array}{r} 5 \\ \times\ 8 \\ \hline \end{array}$$

$$\frac{4}{5} = \frac{16}{—}$$

$$\frac{18}{9} =$$

$$\frac{5}{8} = \frac{25}{—}$$

$$\frac{2}{7} = \frac{}{21}$$

$$35 \div 7 =$$

$$\begin{array}{r} 25 \\ -\ 6 \\ \hline \end{array}$$

$$\begin{array}{r} 11 \\ +\ 5 \\ \hline \end{array}$$

$$7\overline{)28}\ =$$

$$\begin{array}{r} 17 \\ -\ 8 \\ \hline \end{array}$$

$$\begin{array}{r} 17 \\ +\ 2 \\ \hline \end{array}$$

$$\frac{6}{2} =$$

$$\frac{7}{13} = \frac{14}{—}$$

$$\begin{array}{r} 20 \\ -\ 9 \\ \hline \end{array}$$

$$2\overline{)16}\ =$$

$$\frac{8}{11} = \frac{24}{—}$$

$$\begin{array}{r} 3 \\ +\ 6 \\ \hline \end{array}$$

$$\begin{array}{r} 9 \\ \times\ 4 \\ \hline \end{array}$$

$$\begin{array}{r} 6 \\ \times\ 5 \\ \hline \end{array}$$

$$\begin{array}{r} 7 \\ +\ 7 \\ \hline \end{array}$$

$$\begin{array}{r} 16 \\ -\ 5 \\ \hline \end{array}$$

$$\begin{array}{r} 7 \\ \times\ 7 \\ \hline \end{array}$$

$$\begin{array}{r} 26 \\ -\ 2 \\ \hline \end{array}$$

$$\frac{6}{9} = \frac{2}{—}$$

$$\begin{array}{r} 8 \\ \times\ 4 \\ \hline \end{array}$$

$$\frac{40}{4} =$$

$$\frac{9}{15} = \frac{27}{—}$$

$$4\overline{)28}\ =$$

$$\begin{array}{r} 4 \\ +\ 4 \\ \hline \end{array}$$

$$\frac{3}{4} = \frac{15}{—}$$

$$\begin{array}{r} 24 \\ -12 \\ \hline \end{array}$$

$$\begin{array}{r} 9 \\ \times\ 6 \\ \hline \end{array}$$

$$30 \div 6 =$$

$$\frac{1}{4} = \frac{6}{—}$$

$$\begin{array}{r} 6 \\ \times\ 9 \\ \hline \end{array}$$

$$\frac{1}{3} = \frac{7}{\quad}$$

$$48 \div 6 =$$

$$\begin{array}{r} 9 \\ \times\ 8 \\ \hline \end{array}$$

$$\begin{array}{r} 8 \\ \times\ 2 \\ \hline \end{array}$$

$$\begin{array}{r} 5 \\ +\ 7 \\ \hline \end{array}$$

$$\begin{array}{r} 5 \\ \times\ 5 \\ \hline \end{array}$$

$$\frac{8}{9} = \frac{\quad}{72}$$

$$\frac{36}{6} =$$

$$\frac{1}{10} = \frac{3}{\quad}$$

$$\frac{2}{7} = \frac{14}{\quad}$$

$$24 \div 3 =$$

$$\begin{array}{r} 25 \\ -\ 4 \\ \hline \end{array}$$

$$\begin{array}{r} 15 \\ +\ 2 \\ \hline \end{array}$$

$$6\overline{)42}\ =$$

$$\begin{array}{r} 12 \\ -\ 5 \\ \hline \end{array}$$

$$\begin{array}{r} 3 \\ +\ 7 \\ \hline \end{array}$$

$$\frac{42}{7} =$$

$$\frac{6}{15} = \frac{\quad}{5}$$

$$\begin{array}{r} 23 \\ -\ 5 \\ \hline \end{array}$$

$$7\overline{)35}\ =$$

$$\frac{5}{6} = \frac{20}{\quad}$$

$$\begin{array}{r} 6 \\ +\ 6 \\ \hline \end{array}$$

$$\begin{array}{r} 7 \\ \times\ 4 \\ \hline \end{array}$$

$$\begin{array}{r} 9 \\ \times\ 9 \\ \hline \end{array}$$

$$\begin{array}{r} 8 \\ +\ 8 \\ \hline \end{array}$$

$$\begin{array}{r} 10 \\ -\ 6 \\ \hline \end{array}$$

$$\begin{array}{r} 4 \\ \times\ 4 \\ \hline \end{array}$$

$$\begin{array}{r} 18 \\ -\ 5 \\ \hline \end{array}$$

$$\frac{4}{5} = \frac{20}{\quad}$$

$$\begin{array}{r} 7 \\ \times\ 6 \\ \hline \end{array}$$

$$\frac{18}{6} =$$

$$\frac{7}{8} = \frac{\quad}{64}$$

$$5\overline{)35}\ =$$

$$\begin{array}{r} 6 \\ +\ 7 \\ \hline \end{array}$$

$$\frac{9}{14} = \frac{18}{\quad}$$

$$\begin{array}{r} 14 \\ -\ 6 \\ \hline \end{array}$$

$$\begin{array}{r} 8 \\ \times\ 4 \\ \hline \end{array}$$

$$16 \div 4 =$$

$$\frac{3}{8} = \frac{15}{\quad}$$

$\begin{array}{r} 7 \\ \times\ 6 \\ \hline \end{array}$
$\dfrac{\quad}{\quad} = \dfrac{21}{42}$
$12 \div 3 =$
$\begin{array}{r} 7 \\ \times\ 9 \\ \hline \end{array}$
$\begin{array}{r} 8 \\ \times\ 8 \\ \hline \end{array}$

$\begin{array}{r} 9 \\ +\ 8 \\ \hline \end{array}$
$\begin{array}{r} 1 \\ \times\ 1 \\ \hline \end{array}$
$\dfrac{\quad}{\quad} = \dfrac{3}{9}$
$\dfrac{16}{8} =$
$\dfrac{6}{13} = \dfrac{\quad}{26}$

$\dfrac{4}{7} = \dfrac{28}{\quad}$
$8 \div 1 =$
$\begin{array}{r} 19 \\ -\ 4 \\ \hline \end{array}$
$\begin{array}{r} 8 \\ +\ 7 \\ \hline \end{array}$
$8\overline{)24} =$

$\begin{array}{r} 15 \\ -\ 7 \\ \hline \end{array}$
$\begin{array}{r} 18 \\ +\ 2 \\ \hline \end{array}$
$\dfrac{35}{5} =$
$\dfrac{7}{9} = \dfrac{\quad}{63}$
$\begin{array}{r} 8 \\ -\ 3 \\ \hline \end{array}$

$2\overline{)10} =$
$\dfrac{2}{5} = \dfrac{8}{\quad}$
$\begin{array}{r} 6 \\ +\ 5 \\ \hline \end{array}$
$\begin{array}{r} 6 \\ \times\ 4 \\ \hline \end{array}$
$\begin{array}{r} 7 \\ \times\ 2 \\ \hline \end{array}$

$\begin{array}{r} 13 \\ +\ 7 \\ \hline \end{array}$
$\begin{array}{r} 31 \\ -\ 3 \\ \hline \end{array}$
$\begin{array}{r} 7 \\ \times\ 7 \\ \hline \end{array}$
$\begin{array}{r} 27 \\ -\ 6 \\ \hline \end{array}$
$\dfrac{7}{8} = \dfrac{\quad}{56}$

$\begin{array}{r} 8 \\ \times\ 3 \\ \hline \end{array}$
$\dfrac{9}{3} =$
$\dfrac{3}{5} = \dfrac{\quad}{35}$
$7\overline{)42} =$
$\begin{array}{r} 14 \\ +\ 14 \\ \hline \end{array}$

$\dfrac{\quad}{\quad} = \dfrac{4}{40}$
$\begin{array}{r} 15 \\ -\ 7 \\ \hline \end{array}$
$\begin{array}{r} 9 \\ \times\ 8 \\ \hline \end{array}$
$48 \div 6 =$
$\dfrac{6}{\quad} = \dfrac{36}{42}$

# ADDITIONAL RESOURCES

QR Code Worksheets Download          QR Code Answer Key Download

The QR codes above will provide you with access to digital worksheets that you may download and print in addition to the answer key for each week's quiz. The answer key can also be found on our website, www.LtoJ.net, on our free resources page. All printed and digital materials are protected by copywright law.

## LOOKING FOR ADDITIONAL GRADE LEVELS?

Math Fluency Quizzes:          Math Standards Quizzes:

*Kindergarten*                    *Kindergarten*

*Grade 1*                        *Grade 1*

*Grade 2*                        *Grade 2*

*Grade 3*                        *Grade 3*

*Grade 4*                        *Grade 4*

*Grade 5*                        *Grade 5*

*Grade 6*                        *Grade 6*

*Grade 7*                        *Grade 7*

*Grade 8*                        *Grade 8*

                            *Algebra I*

                            *Algebra II*

# Do you have a great photo or video of your student using one of our products?

We would love the opportunity to share it on our website and social media channels!

Email us at info@ltoj.net

If you have a story to share, we would also like to hear from you. We feature student stories during presentations and on our social media accounts.

Our team loves sharing the joy of a child understanding new concepts. It allows our audience to experience firsthand the mission our team works towards every day; for students to maintain the same love of learning they brought to Kindergarten throughout all their years of schooling and into adulthood.

Thank you for being a loyal customer. We appreciate you!

**The LtoJ Team**

*Follow us on Instagram, Facebook, TikTok and YouTube*
*@LtoJLLC*

# ABOUT THE AUTHORS

**Peggy McLean** is a Math Specialist for elementary age students. She has traveled across the United States training teachers with the use of manipulative materials to build understanding of mathematical concepts. She knows that teachers must first experience the joy of learning and discovering themselves so that they can share this enthusiasm with children. She says, "Teaching is posing problems more than telling students how to do it."

She holds both Bachelor's and Master's degrees from California State University, San Jose. She taught math, science, and social studies courses for pre-service teachers at Notre Dame de Namur University for 25 years.

Peggy was the Elementary Math Specialist at Nueva School for 45 years and has held the same position at Synapse School for the past 8 years. Peggy's expertise in teaching mathematics is well known by audiences at National Council of Teachers of Mathematics conferences as well as those who were fortunate to learn from her in local school district staff development workshops. Educators who hear that Peggy's books are being updated and published for classroom and home education use express joy that her genius work is still available for a new generation of children. Peggy calls San Carlos, California home.

---

**Dr. Lyle Lee Jenkins** is an author, speaker, and recognized authority in improving educational outcomes. He believes that implementing a growth mindset and celebrating progress are the keys to helping students learn more and retain their enthusiasm for school.

His education experience, that spans over 50 years, ranges from working as a teacher, a principal, and a school superintendent in the California School System to being a University Professor. In 2003, Lyle Lee founded LtoJ, LLC hoping to impact and guide the way we approach education.

Lyle Lee Jenkins has authored six books showcasing continuous improvement in schools, including *How to Create a Perfect School*, *Optimize Your School*, *Permission to Forget*, *From Systems Thinking to Systemic Action*, *Improving Student Learning*, and *How to Create a Perfect Home School*. All of his books offer powerful, practical suggestions for every aspect of education. The two most influential people supporting Dr. Jenkins's work are W. Edwards Deming and John Hattie.

Having spoken to educators all across the United States, Latin America, Europe, Australia, and Asia, Lyle Lee Jenkins is passionate about equipping the next generation with a true love of learning.

Dr. Lyle Lee Jenkins holds a Bachelor of Arts degree from Point Loma Nazarene University, a Masters of Education from San Jose State University and a Ph.D. from the Claremont Graduate University.

*Lyle Lee Jenkins's website, www.LtoJ.net, is a great place to discover useful tools to guide your educational journey.*

Made in the USA
Middletown, DE
27 February 2023

25631336R00044